AFTER HIGH SCHOOL COMES COLLEGE...

Frank Nardelli

With Foreword By Damen Lopez

Illustrated by Danny Moore

MASCOT BOOKS

www.mascotbooks.com

Foreword

It was such a simple event. As my mother shared with me the same words that grace the cover of this book, "after high school comes college," she did so with calm confidence and matter of fact conviction. She didn't need to be overly passionate or demanding in her words to me, she just needed to be consistent. You see, it wasn't these five words that inspired my brother and I to become the first college grads in our family, it was the fact that we heard these words every single night.

The act of telling our children that college is in their future should be as second nature as our expression of love for them. There's no need for theatrics, and no demand for artful persuasion. Just a simple, guided, and certain belief in your child's ability to achieve a level of academic success that far too many do not. It will take years and there may even be a few bumps along the road, but your sons and daughters will someday participate in higher education that will open the door to an abundance of opportunity. As they get older, they will thank you for your simple affirmation.

— Damen Lopez
Founder, No Excuses University

"Dan! You said it would be my turn! You said if I swept the floor last night I could stack the cans on the shelves tonight! That's what you said!"

"Okay, Damen," said Dan. "How about I help you sweep the floor and then we will stack the cans together?"

"Deal!" yelled Damen and the two young brothers high-fived.

Damen and Dan were two boys with an important job. Even though Damen was only in third grade and Dan was in fifth grade, the boys worked every night after school helping their mom and dad clean a grocery store in the small town where they lived. Each night, their family would come downstairs from the small apartment they lived in on the second floor over the grocery store.

Damen and Dan's parents were hard workers, but times were tough. When they were offered to live in the apartment above the grocery store in exchange for cleaning it every night, their parents accepted.

The boys went to school all day, only to rush home to complete their homework. Their mom and dad would come home from their day jobs and the family would have dinner together. As soon as the dishes from dinner were cleared from the table, off they went down the stairs to clean the store. When they finished cleaning, Damen was usually so tired he could barely keep his eyes open. Even though she was probably more tired than Damen could understand, every night his mom, Barbara, would tuck him and his brother into their beds. As she gave them a kiss, her words were always the same. "After high school comes college, Damen. After high school comes college, Dan."

"I know mom," Damen would reply. "I love you." As his mom turned off the light in the boys' bedroom and shut the door, Damen turned over and stared across the darkness to his brother, Dan, who was lying in his bed trying to fall asleep. "Dan? Dan? Are you still awake? Why do you think mom says that to us every night? Why do you think she tells us every night that after high school comes college? I know what comes after high school!"

"Maybe that's why she tells us, you knucklehead. Maybe you know it because she tells us every night. Now be quiet and go to sleep!"

So Damen would lay there...quiet in the dark...staring at the ceiling...watching the lights from the traffic on the street below flash across the walls. He would listen to himself breathe, and he would begin to dream...

"Damen! Damen! Are you listening to me? I'm trying to give you some advice, but I don't think you are even listening to me!"

"I'm sorry, Fran. I was listening. I think you are going to be great! I think you will be able to help a lot of people."

Damen had been friends with Fran ever since they were in kindergarten. Fran was one of the smartest people that Damen knew. She wanted to be a counselor. Fran wanted to go to the University of Southern California, which wasn't too far from the little town were Fran and Damen grew up. This was one of the universities that Damen's mom talked about. They called this school U.S.C. and U.S.C. was a big college. Lots of men and women were students there. His friend Fran read in a book that she could learn how to be a counselor at U.S.C., so she decided that she wanted to go to college there. Damen knew a few things about U.S.C. He knew their mascot was a Trojan, and he knew their sports teams wore maroon and gold.

"Fran, I know you are smart enough, but are you sure a kid like you from a small town can go to a big college like U.S.C.? Do you really think we can go to college?"

"I do, Damen, I really do! Mr. Pen told us we should dream BIG! He said there are no limits to how smart and successful we can be. I think we can do it!"

"Mr. Pen" was what Damen and Fran called their teacher, Mr. Penasquitos. He was a great teacher, and he always told Damen's class that what they were learning in elementary school was just the beginning of their education.

"Hey, Nick! Fran says she's going to U.S.C. Are you going to college, too?" asked Damen.

"Of course I'm going to college, Damen! I want to go to the University of Nebraska. I want to learn how to be a leader. Maybe I can be a mayor, or a governor, or even a senator some day. I want to learn how to lead so I can help a lot of people, too!" said Nick.

When they were in first grade, Nick's family moved into Damen's town from Chicago. Nick was the first kid that Damen ever met from some place away from where he grew up. Nick and Damen quickly became good friends, and Damen knew Nick would make a great leader some day.

"I want to go to Nebraska," Nick said. "I read a newspaper article about our mayor. He does a great job, and he went to the University of Nebraska. I'm going to go to college there too so I can learn how to be a good leader like he is. Go Huskers!"

"I would vote for you, Nick!" said Damen. "Hey, Doug!" Damen called out to his friend who walked onto the schoolyard as Nick and Damen were talking. "How's it going?"

Doug was very tall, and he loved math. "What are you guys talking about? Do you want to play some basketball?"asked Doug. "I just measured how tall I am, and I'm almost 5 feet 10 inches now! Pretty soon I will be six feet tall and you know what that means? I'll be able to jump high enough to dunk this basketball!"

"Doug, do you ever stop playing around with numbers? Yesterday, you told us how much the basketball weighed. We were just talking about going to college. Fran says she's going to U.S.C. because she wants to learn how to be a counselor. Nick is going to Nebraska because he wants to learn how to be a leader. Are you going to college, Doug?" asked Damen even though he could guess what Doug's answer would be.

"Hook 'em horns! You bet I'm going to college! I'm going to Texas, man! Why do you think I'm wearing this burnt orange shirt?" yelled Doug poking himself proudly in his chest.

"Doug, we are in third grade! How do you know you are going to Texas? We are still kids!" said Damen.

"I am going to the University of Texas because that's where I want to go to college. It doesn't matter how old we are. Kids can have dreams just like grown ups can. My mom went to the University of Texas, and she took us there one summer when we visited my aunt. It was awesome, and they have a great basketball team! If I practice a lot, I bet I can get a scholarship and they will pay for my tuition."

Damen wanted to pretend like he knew what Doug was talking about, but his curiosity was too strong to resist. "Tuition? What is a tuition?" asked Damen.

"It costs money to go to college," said Doug. "You learn a lot when you go there but you have to pay for the classes you take. Every college has its own tuition. The prices are different depending on where you go."

"Some schools cost a lot of money and some less. If you get a scholarship, then you won't have to pay as much or sometimes you won't have to pay anything at all!"

"He's right, Damen," said Fran. "My older sister has a friend who got all A's in high school, and she got a scholarship to go to the University of Florida! They paid for her classes, her food, and even paid for her dorm room. She didn't have to pay for anything because her grades were so good in high school."

"Florida? I love that school and the Gators!" said Damen. He stretched out his arms and yelled, "Chomp! Chomp! Chomp!"

Damen's friend Frank, who started to play basketball with Doug as Fran was talking, laughed at Damen. "That's a good one, Damen! You make one scary Gator!"

"Frank! I didn't know you were back. I thought you went to Michigan with your mom." Frank's mom was a reading teacher at Damen's school. Her class was covered by a substitute teacher this week because she went to a teachers' conference in Detroit.

"We just got back last night. My mom said she learned a lot," explained Frank. "We saw the Big House! It was so cool!"

"What's the Big House?" asked Damen.

"The Big House is the football stadium at the University of Michigan. It's huge. We took a tour of the University of Michigan in Ann Arbor when we were in the Detroit area. I really liked it. My mom is thinking about going to graduate school there for her doctorate."

"Graduate school? Doctorate?" Damen asked as he held his hands up in disbelief. "I thought once you graduated from college you didn't have to go to school anymore?"

"Nobody knows everything, Damen," Frank explained. "You can always learn more. My mom has been teaching a long time but she said she wants to earn her doctorate degree because she has some questions about how to teach kids how to read. She went to college but now she wants to learn more. After college, if you want to learn more, you can go to graduate school."

"We were talking about going to college before you got here. Frank, do you want to go to college?" asked Damen.

"I am going to college! My mom and dad told my sister and me, college is like 13th grade. You know how you go to high school until you're a senior and that's 12th grade? My mom and dad told us we don't stop going to school in 12th grade. We have to go college after high school and go to 13th, 14th, 15th, and 16th grade!"

"16th grade! That's hilarious! Who ever heard of 16th grade?" Damen laughed as he asked the question.

Frank passed the basketball back to Doug, and Doug stopped and put the basketball on his hip. "College usually takes four years to finish, Damen. What Frank is saying sounds funny, but he's right. You leave high school and you attend college for four years."

"I know, I know" said Damen. "My mom tells me and my brother every night—'after high school comes college. After high school comes college!' How do I know if I can go to college? We don't have a lot of money. I'm not great at math like Doug, and I don't know people who have gone to college like Fran. I don't know if I'm smart enough..."

"DAMEN!" Fran, Nick, Doug, and Frank yelled out Damen's name together to stop him before he went any further.

Fran was the first to speak. "Stop making excuses, Damen! You heard what Mr. Pen said. Dream BIG! Believe in yourself!"

"Come on, Damen," said Nick. "We all have things we are not good at, but that's no excuse."

"That's right, Damen! You deserve to go to college just as much as we do," said Frank as he patted Damen on the shoulder.

"Wow!" admitted Damen. "You guys are right. I am making excuses. We ALL deserve to go to college! We do! We deserve to go college. Every kid does...every kid does...every child deserves the chance to go to college!"

"Damen! Damen, wake up knucklehead! Wake up! We've got to go to school!" Dan said shaking Damen's shoulder trying to wake him.

"Huh? What? Was I dreaming? Dan! Mom's right! We have to go college! Mom's right, Dan!"

"Of course she's right little brother! You can't go to college until you finish the third grade, and after that you have to go to fourth grade. If you keep working hard you will get there and so will I!" said Dan as he lifted his backpack on his shoulder and put on his U.S.C. ballcap.

"Come on, Dan! We better go! We can't make excuses! We need to dream BIG!"

"Damen! Wait! Damen! You're still in your pajamas, knucklehead! We have to go to school but not in our pajamas! Wait! Damen!"

About No Excuses University

No Excuses University is a network of elementary, middle, and junior high schools across the United States. These schools actively promote a comprehensive model of college readiness to all students the moment they begin elementary school. Every No Excuses University has a well-defined process for identifying and creating the six exceptional systems of a culture of universal achievement, collaboration, standards alignment, assessment, data analysis and interventions. In addition, every No Excuses University campus works diligently to expose students to powerful college symbolism. This symbolism is seen in the college flags and banners hung on every door, felt though the close partnerships forged between classrooms and universities, and heard in the college chants that exist at each grade level.

For more information about how the No Excuses University endeavor is changing the lives of thousands of students across the country, visit www.noexcusesu.com.

About the Author

Frank P. Nardelli II resides in Livonia, Michigan with his wife, Shana, two daughters, Annalin and Callie, and their dog, Buddy. Born in Plattsburgh, New York, Frank is the son of Anna and Frank Nardelli. Frank earned his Bachelor of Science in Education from S.U.N.Y. Geneseo, his Master of Arts in Literacy Education at the University of Michigan, and is earning his Education Specialist in Administration and Supervision degree at Wayne State University. In 1997, Frank joined the founding faculty of Dove Academy. Frank has served the Dove Academy community over the last 13 years as a first grade teacher, third grade teacher, assistant principal and principal. The 2009 – 2010 school year was Frank's sixth year as the principal of Dove. In the 2007 – 2008 school year, Frank was a finalist for the Michigan Association of Public School Academies' Administrator of the Year Award. Phi Delta Kappa International has recognized him as a 2009 – 2010 Emerging Leader in Education and S.U.N.Y. Geneseo has awarded Frank their 2010 Excellence in Education Award.

Frank is also the author of a children's book about Dove Academy, *We Love the Dove*, published by Mascot Books in the fall of 2009. Frank appreciates the opportunity to work with the students, families, and staff of Dove Academy. He is passionate about Dove's No Excuses University Program and is proud to share Dove Academy's story with other schools and educators at Turnaround Schools Institutes throughout the country.

He can be contacted through Dove Academy's main office at (313) 366-9110 or by email at fnardelli@doveacademy.net.

No Excuses University Network of Schools

- Abbott Middle School
- Agua Caliente
- Bahia Vista School
- Bond Elementary School
- Bruce Vento Elementary School
- Central Road School
- Cielo Vista Elementary School
- Clark Elementary School
- Devonshire School
- Don Pedro Elementary School
- Dove Academy
- Ellis Middle School
- Emerson Elementary School
- First Philadelphia Charter School of Literacy
- Fox Elementary School
- Frank C. Whiteley Elementary School

- Genesee Elementary School
- Gray M. Sanborn School
- Hanover Countryside Elementary School
- Hanover Highlands Elementary School
- Harvest Valley Elementary School
- Hemet Elementary School
- Highgrove Elementary School
- Highland Elementary School
- Hollingworth Elementary School
- Home Gardens Elementary School
- H.T. Jaramillo Community
- Jane Addams School
- Jane Stenson Elementary School
- John Muir Literacy Academy

- Juniper Elementary School
- Karshner Elementary School
- Kenyon Woods Middle School
- Killybrooke Elementary School
- Kyrene de los Ninos
- Lake Louise Elementary School
- Lake View Elementary School
- Landau Elementary School
- Liberty Elementary School
- Lincoln Elementary School
- Los Penasquitos Elementary School
- Lowrie Elementary School
- Mann Middle School
- Mango Elementary School
- Meadows Union Elementary School
- Mesa Verde Elementary School
- Moffitt Elementary School
- Nash Elementary School
- Old Orchard Junior High School
- Olive Elementary School
- Orchard Place Elementary School
- Prince Elementary School
- Rio Vista Elementary School
- Roosevelt Elementary School
- Rosemary Kennedy Elementary School
- Sam Houston Middle School
- San Jacinto Elementary School
- Stokoe Elementary School
- Thomas Elementary School
- Thomas Jefferson School
- Thurston Elementary School
- Travis Middle School
- Vermont Elementary School
- Virginia Lake School
- Voorhis Elementary School
- Wakefield Elementary School
- Washington Elementary School
- Washington Terrace Elementary School
- Whittier Elementary School
- Willie E. Williams Elementary School
- Willow Bend School
- Winston Campus Elementary School

This book was written as a tribute to my Mom and Dad, Anna and Frank Nardelli. Not only did they provide me with my college education, they set the expectation for me to go to college at an early age. I hope this book honors you as a small token of my appreciation for all of your love and support. In addition, this book is dedicated to my wife, Shana Lynn Nardelli. Thank you for believing in me through all of the phases of our lives. I love you.

~ Frank Nardelli

For Charlie and Toofer. ~ Danny Moore

www.mascotbooks.com

For more information, please contact:
Mascot Books
P.O. Box 220157
Chantilly, VA 20153-0157
info@mascotbooks.com

ISBN: 1-936319-02-0
CPSIA Code: PRT0510A

Printed in the United States

Baseball

Boston Red Sox	Hello, *Wally*!	Jerry Remy
Boston Red Sox	*Wally The Green Monster And His Journey Through Red Sox Nation!*	Jerry Remy
Boston Red Sox	Coast to Coast with *Wally The Green Monster*	Jerry Remy
Boston Red Sox	A Season with *Wally The Green Monster*	Jerry Remy
Colorado Rockies	Hello, *Dinger*!	Aimee Aryal
Detroit Tigers	Hello, *Paws*!	Aimee Aryal
New York Yankees	Let's Go, *Yankees*!	Yogi Berra
New York Yankees	*Yankees* Town	Aimee Aryal
New York Mets	Hello, *Mr. Met*!	Rusty Staub
New York Mets	*Mr. Met* and his Journey Through the Big Apple	Aimee Aryal
St. Louis Cardinals	Hello, *Fredbird*!	Ozzie Smith
Philadelphia Phillies	Hello, *Phillie Phanatic*!	Aimee Aryal
Chicago Cubs	Let's Go, *Cubs*!	Aimee Aryal
Chicago White Sox	Let's Go, *White Sox*!	Aimee Aryal
Cleveland Indians	Hello, *Slider*!	Bob Feller
Seattle Mariners	Hello, *Mariner Moose*!	Aimee Aryal
Washington Nationals	Hello, *Screech*!	Aimee Aryal
Milwaukee Brewers	Hello, *Bernie Brewer*!	Aimee Aryal

College

Alabama	Hello, Big Al!	Aimee Aryal
Alabama	Roll Tide!	Ken Stabler
Alabama	Big Al's Journey Through the Yellowhammer State	Aimee Aryal
Arizona	Hello, Wilbur!	Lute Olson
Arizona State	Hello, Sparky!	Aimee Aryal
Arkansas	Hello, Big Red!	Aimee Aryal
Arkansas	Big Red's Journey Through the Razorback State	Aimee Aryal
Auburn	Hello, Aubie!	Aimee Aryal
Auburn	War Eagle!	Pat Dye
Auburn	Aubie's Journey Through the Yellowhammer State	Aimee Aryal
Boston College	Hello, Baldwin!	Aimee Aryal
Brigham Young	Hello, Cosmo!	LaVell Edwards
Cal - Berkeley	Hello, Oski!	Aimee Aryal
Clemson	Hello, Tiger!	Aimee Aryal
Clemson	Tiger's Journey Through the Palmetto State	Aimee Aryal
Colorado	Hello, Ralphie!	Aimee Aryal
Connecticut	Hello, Jonathan!	Aimee Aryal
Duke	Hello, Blue Devil!	Aimee Aryal
Florida	Hello, Albert!	Aimee Aryal
Florida	Albert's Journey Through the Sunshine State	Aimee Aryal
Florida State	Let's Go, 'Noles!	Aimee Aryal
Georgia	Hello, Hairy Dawg!	Aimee Aryal
Georgia	How 'Bout Them Dawgs!	Vince Dooley
Georgia	Hairy Dawg's Journey Through the Peach State	Vince Dooley
Georgia Tech	Hello, Buzz!	Aimee Aryal
Gonzaga	Spike, The Gonzaga Bulldog	Mike Pringle
Illinois	Let's Go, Illini!	Aimee Aryal
Indiana	Let's Go, Hoosiers!	Aimee Aryal
Iowa	Hello, Herky!	Aimee Aryal
Iowa State	Hello, Cy!	Amy DeLashmutt
James Madison	Hello, Duke Dog!	Aimee Aryal
Kansas	Hello, Big Jay!	Aimee Aryal
Kansas State	Hello, Willie!	Dan Walter
Kentucky	Hello, Wildcat!	Aimee Aryal
LSU	Hello, Mike!	Aimee Aryal
LSU	Mike's Journey Through the Bayou State	Aimee Aryal
Maryland	Hello, Testudo!	Aimee Aryal
Michigan	Let's Go, Blue!	Aimee Aryal
Michigan State	Hello, Sparty!	Aimee Aryal
Michigan State	Sparty's Journey Through Michigan	Aimee Aryal
Middle Tennessee	Hello, Lightning!	Aimee Aryal
Minnesota	Hello, Goldy!	Aimee Aryal
Mississippi	Hello, Colonel Rebel!	Aimee Aryal

Pro Football

Carolina Panthers	Let's Go, Panthers!	Aimee Aryal
Chicago Bears	Let's Go, Bears!	Aimee Aryal
Dallas Cowboys	How 'Bout Them Cowboys!	Aimee Aryal
Green Bay Packers	Go, Pack, Go!	Aimee Aryal
Kansas City Chiefs	Let's Go, Chiefs!	Aimee Aryal
Minnesota Vikings	Let's Go, Vikings!	Aimee Aryal
New York Giants	Let's Go, Giants!	Aimee Aryal
New York Jets	J-E-T-S! Jets, Jets, Jets!	Aimee Aryal
New England Patriots	Let's Go, Patriots!	Aimee Aryal
Pittsburg Steelers	Here We Go, Steelers!	Aimee Aryal
Seattle Seahawks	Let's Go, Seahawks!	Aimee Aryal
Washington Redskins	Hail To The Redskins!	Aimee Aryal

Basketball

Dallas Mavericks	Let's Go, Mavs!	Mark Cuban
Boston Celtics	Let's Go, Celtics!	Aimee Aryal

Other

Kentucky Derby	White Diamond Runs For The Roses	Aimee Aryal
Marine Corps Marathon	Run, Miles, Run!	Aimee Aryal
Mississippi State	Hello, Bully!	Aimee Aryal
Missouri	Hello, Truman!	Todd Donoho
Missouri	Hello, Truman! Show Me Missouri!	Todd Donoho
Nebraska	Hello, Herbie Husker!	Aimee Aryal
North Carolina	Hello, Rameses!	Aimee Aryal
North Carolina	Rameses' Journey Through the Tar Heel State	Aimee Aryal
North Carolina St.	Hello, Mr. Wuf!	Aimee Aryal
North Carolina St.	Mr. Wuf's Journey Through North Carolina	Aimee Aryal
Northern Arizona	Hello, Louie!	Jeanette S. Bake
Notre Dame	Let's Go, Irish!	Aimee Aryal
Ohio State	Hello, Brutus!	Aimee Aryal
Ohio State	Brutus' Journey	Aimee Aryal
Oklahoma	Let's Go, Sooners!	Aimee Aryal
Oklahoma State	Hello, Pistol Pete!	Aimee Aryal
Oregon	Go Ducks!	Aimee Aryal
Oregon State	Hello, Benny the Beaver!	Aimee Aryal
Penn State	Hello, Nittany Lion!	Aimee Aryal
Penn State	We Are Penn State!	Joe Paterno
Purdue	Hello, Purdue Pete!	Aimee Aryal
Rutgers	Hello, Scarlet Knight!	Aimee Aryal
South Carolina	Hello, Cocky!	Aimee Aryal
South Carolina	Cocky's Journey Through the Palmetto State	Aimee Aryal
So. California	Hello, Tommy Trojan!	Aimee Aryal
Syracuse	Hello, Otto!	Aimee Aryal
Tennessee	Hello, Smokey!	Aimee Aryal
Tennessee	Smokey's Journey Through the Volunteer State	Aimee Aryal
Texas	Hello, Hook 'Em!	Aimee Aryal
Texas	Hook 'Em's Journey Through the Lone Star State	Aimee Aryal
Texas A & M	Howdy, Reveille!	Aimee Aryal
Texas A & M	Reveille's Journey Through the Lone Star State	Aimee Aryal
Texas Tech	Hello, Masked Rider!	Aimee Aryal
UCLA	Hello, Joe Bruin!	Aimee Aryal
Virginia	Hello, CavMan!	Aimee Aryal
Virginia Tech	Hello, Hokie Bird!	Aimee Aryal
Virginia Tech	Yea, It's Hokie Game Day!	Frank Beamer
Virginia Tech	Hokie Bird's Journey Through Virginia	Aimee Aryal
Wake Forest	Hello, Demon Deacon!	Aimee Aryal
Washington	Hello, Harry the Husky!	Aimee Aryal
Washington State	Hello, Butch!	Aimee Aryal
West Virginia	Hello, Mountaineer!	Aimee Aryal
West Virginia	The Mountaineer's Journey Through West Virginia	Leslie H. Haning
Wisconsin	Hello, Bucky!	Aimee Aryal
Wisconsin	Bucky's Journey Through the Badger State	Aimee Aryal

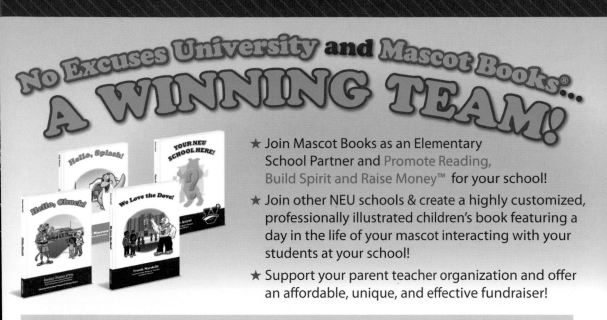